M000229424

JUST BE GLAD

BY
CHRISTIAN D. LARSON

1912
THE NEW LITERATURE PUBLISHING COMPANY
LOS ANGELES, CALIFORNIA

COPYRIGHT 1912
BY
Christian D. Larson

LL things respond to the call of rejoicing; all things gather where life is a song.

This is the message of the new order, the new life and the new time. It is the golden text of the great gospel of human sunshine. It is the central truth of that sublime philosophy of existence, which declares that the greatest good is happiness, and that heaven is here and now.

To live in the spirit of this wonderful message; to be a living example of this great gospel, to work out in everyday life the principle of this inspiring philosophy, the first and most important thing to do, is to lay aside our sorrows and glooms, and just be glad.

Wherever you are, or whatever has happened, just be glad. Be glad because you are here. You are here in a beautiful world; and all that is beauti-

ful may be found in this world. It is
a world wherein all that is rich in life
may be enjoyed beyond measure;
a world wherein happiness may overflow eternally in every human heart; a
world wherein all the dreams of life
may be realized, and all the visions of
the soul made true. Then why should
we not be glad; first of all, that we are
here; that we are in this world; that
we may stay here for a long time if we
so desire, and enjoy every minute to
the full.

The real truth is that this world is
nothing less than a limitless sea of
happiness, the vastness and glory of
which we are just beginning to know.
And life itself is a song, while time is
one eternal symphony. To be in tune
with life, therefore, and to be in harmony with the endless music of time,
we must of necessity be glad. But
after we have learned to be glad,

under every circumstance, it is no
longer a necessity; it is a privilege,
and has become a part of our active,
living, thinking self.

Just be glad, and you always will
be glad. You will have better reason
to be glad. You will have more and
more things to make you glad. For
great is the power of sunshine, espe-
cially human sunshine. It can change
anything, transform anything, re-make
anything, and cause anything to become as fair and beautiful as itself.

Just be glad and your fate will
change; a new life will begin and a
new future will dawn for you. All
things that are good and desirable
will begin to come into your world in
greater measure, and you will be en-
riched far beyond your expectations,
both from the without and from the
within. And the cause of the change
is this, that all things respond to the

call of rejoicing; all things gather where life is a song.

When you are tempted to feel discouraged or disappointed, be glad instead. Know that you can, say that you will, and stand uncompromisingly upon your resolve. Be strong and be glad. For when strength and rejoicing combine in your soul, every trace of gloom or despair must disappear; because such conditions can exist only where weakness is the rule and mastery the exception.

Combine strength with rejoicing and you will exercise a magic power— you will possess a secret that will serve you royally no matter what your difficulties or obstacles may be. All joy is light; and it is the light that dispels the darkness.

When things are not to your liking, be glad nevertheless, for the glad heart can cause all things to be as we wish them to be. When things do not give you pleasure, proceed instead to create pleasure in your own heart and soul. And you can if you will always be glad. Besides, things will soon change for the better if you continue in the spirit of rejoicing. It is the law that all good things will sooner or later come and be, where the greatest happiness is to be found. Therefore, be happiness in yourself, regardless of times, seasons or circumstances.

When things do not please you, resolve to please yourself by being glad, and you can add immeasurably to your happiness in this simple manner. Then you must remember that the fountain of joy within your own soul is infinitely greater than all external sources of joy combined. But as far as we can, we should add the joys from without to the joys from within, and in all things be glad.

JUST BE GLAD

Rejoice in your strength, rejoice in your talents and powers, rejoice in the wonders of your own nature. For there is far more in you than you ever dreamed. So whatever may come, you are greater than it all, richer than it all. And knowing this, why should you not be glad.

When evil befalls you, consider the fact that the good that is yet in your possession is many times as great as all the evil you could ever know. Consider this stupendous fact and be glad. Then remember, with rejoicing, that neither evil nor wrong can exist very long in the radiant sunshine of a glad triumphant soul.

If you have lost anything, have no regrets. Be glad and begin again. Be glad that you can begin again. Be glad to know that the future is always richer and better than the past if we only try to make it so. Then forget the loss, and rejoice in the fact that you have the power to secure something far better in return. You know that you have this power; then you can never be otherwise than glad.

Whatever comes or not, sing again and again the song of "the soul victorious"; and mean it with your whole heart. Enter into this song with all the power of mind and spirit, for it is always that which we know and sincerely believe that contains the greater worth and power.

When you resolve to be glad at all times and under every circumstance, resolve also to give your whole heart and soul to the spirit of your rejoicing. Give power to your gladness, and give life to your song. Open the way for all the sunshine of your soul; and see that every sunbeam from within be one of power as well as one of joy.

It is the full joy of the soul that makes the heart young and the mind great. For as it is in nature, so it is also in man. It is the full glory of the noonday sun that quickens the earth, that makes the fields green, that causes the flowers to bloom. Where the sun is strong all growth is luxurious and all nature bountiful. It is the same when the sunshine of the soul is full, strong and constant in the daily life of man. So therefore rejoice with great joy. Rejoice always and give life and power to your joy.

There is magic in the sunshine of the soul; there is a charmed power in the radiant splendor of a beaming countenance. Such a countenance can dispel anything that may threaten to give disappointment or dismay. So remember to be glad and mean it. It is the greatest remedy in the world, and the greatest protector in the world. It can harm nothing for it turns all wrong into right. It is the sunshine from within that causes all darkness to cease to be. It therefore brings good to everybody, and he who is always glad is always adding to the welfare of every member of the race.

When fate seems unkind, do not be unkind to yourself by becoming disheartened or dismayed. Instead, rejoice in the great fact that you are greater and stronger than any fate; that you have the power to master your whole life, and determine your destiny according to your own invincible will. Then resolve that you will begin at once to prove that strength, and cause all the elements of fate to come with you, and work with you, in building for that greater future which you have so often longed for in your visions and dreams.

Therefore, whatever your fate may be, just be glad. You can change it all. And as you proceed to exercise this divine right, the darkness of to-day will become the sunshine of to-morrow, and the disappointments of the present will become the pastures green of the future.

When calamities or catastrophies have overtaken your life, do not think that fate or Providence has ordered it so. Do not think that it has to be. Instead, forget the sorrow and the loss, and congratulate yourself over the fact that you now have the privilege to build for greater things than you ever knew before. Do not weep over loss; but rejoice to think that now you are called upon to prove the greater wisdom and power within you. You have been taken out into a new world. Before you lie vast fields of undeveloped and unexplored opportunities—

fields that you would not have known had not this seeming misfortune come upon you. So count it all joy. All things are working together for a greater good. Now it is for you to come forward in joy and accept the greater good. A richer life and a greater future are in store. Therefore, rejoice and be glad, and give strength to your rejoicing. Let your soul repeat again and again that sweet re-assuring refrain—just be glad. In that refrain there is comfort and peace; it lifts the burdens, removes the clouds, dispels the gloom; it takes away the sadness and the loss, and all is well again. And naturally so, for **all things respond to the call of rejoicing; all things gather where life is a song.**

There is more to live for than you ever imagined. Thus far most of us have only touched the merest surface of human existence; we are only on the verge of the splendor of life as it is; we are standing on the outside, so to speak, of the real mansion of mind and soul; and one reason is we live too much in the limitations of our disappointments, our lost opportunities, our blasted hopes, our vanquished dreams. We remain in that small world, deploring fate, when, if we would only permit mind and soul to take wings and go out upon the vastness of real existence, we would find, not only freedom, but a life infinitely richer than we had ever dreamed.

But if mind and soul are to take wings in this fashion, we must learn to be glad. The heart that lives in disappointments is heavy. It will sink into the lowlands, and remain among the marshes and the bogs. But the glad heart ascends to the mountain tops. Therefore it is when we have such a heart that we can go out in search of new worlds, new opportunities, new possibilities, new joys. And the glad heart always finds that for which it goes in search. The reason is simple; for all things respond to the call of rejoicing; all things gather where life is a song.

The great soul is always in search of ways and means for adding to the welfare of others. But no way is better, greater or more far-reaching than this—just be glad.

Life becomes worth the living only when the living of life makes living more worth while for an ever increasing number. It is only the joys we share that give happiness; it is only the thoughts we express that enrich our own minds; it is only the strength we use in actual helpfulness that makes our own souls strong. Therefore, to add to the pleasures of others, is to add to our own pleasure; to add to the wealth and comfort of others is to add in like manner to our own. This the great soul knows; and every soul is great that has learned to be glad regardless of what may come or go in the world.

To be glad at all times is to be of greater service to mankind than any other thing that we can do. If we have not the power or ability to apply ourselves more tangibly in behalf of others, we can instead be glad. We can always give sunshine. And we shall find that just being glad is frequently sufficient, even when needs seem great and circumstances extreme. In most instances it is all the world wants; but it does want human sunshine so much, that those who can give it at all times need not do anything else to reap immortal fame.

JUST BE GLAD

Surround us with an abundance of human sunshine, and the day's work will easily be done; we shall, with far less effort, overcome our obstacles; our troubles will largely be removed, and our burdens entirely laid aside. Give us the privilege to work to the music of rejoicing and our work will become a pleasure; every duty will become a privilege, and all we do will be well done. This is the way the world thinks and feels. So therefore be glad. Give an abundance of human sunshine everywhere and always, and you will please the world immensely.

Then turn to the home. Can we picture anything more beautiful than a home where every soul therein is a sunbeam; where every countenance is ever lit up with the light of rejoicing; where every word spoken rings with the music of love; and where every thought, uttered or unexpressed, is inspired by the spirit of joy.

It is in such a home that the beautiful, the great and the wonderful in human nature will grow; it is in such a home that our highest ideals will be realized and the divine within find full and resplendent expression. But it is not necessary to describe the pleasures and privileges of such a home; only to say that if you want such a home, just be glad.

Then consider again the worker, and where the workers must gather; what a power for good human sunshine would be in such a place. Consider how all things change when the glad soul arrives, and how all work lightens when the spirit of joy is abroad. And every man has the power to dispense the spirit of joy wherever he may work or live. Every man can ease the ways of others in this remarkable manner;

and the secret is simple—just be glad.

The work you do, be it with mind or muscle, invariably conveys the spirit of your own soul. Therefore work in the spirit of joy and your work will be the product of joy—a rare product —the best of its kind.

It is the man who blends rejoicing with his work who does the best work; it is the man who deeply and sincerely enjoys his work who gives the greatest worth to his work; and the more worth we give to our work the more of the rich and the worthy our work will bring to us.

We realize therefore that it is profitable in every way to learn to be glad. But it is not only profitable to ourselves; also to all others that we may reach through word or deed. Then the profit that comes from the art of being glad is never the result of selfishness. The glad heart is never selfish. The sunbeam does not dance and sing to please its own restricted desire; it does what it does because it is what it is— a happy, carefree sunbeam. It is the same with the glad heart, it sings because it has become the spirit of song; and all are charmed with the song.

No selfish heart can really be glad. No soul that acts solely for personal gain can enter the spirit of joy; and no man who seeks only his own pleasure and comfort can ever take part in the music of rejoicing. And yet, the glad heart receives far more of everything of worth in life than does the one who forgets gladness in pursuit of gain for self alone. And again the answer is simple. For all things respond to the call of rejoicing; all things gather where life is a song.

E glad for the things you have, and you will find you have far more than you thought. Then you will not miss, in the least, the things you have not. Besides, the happier you are over what has come to you, the more and the more will come to you in the future. This is indeed a great secret, and if universally applied would cause want to disappear from the face of the whole earth.

Be glad, for nothing is as serious as it seems to be. Then remember that sunshine can banish any gloom; and you can create in yourself all the sunshine you need; so just be glad.

When trouble and misfortunes surround you, just be glad. The glad heart and the cheerful soul always make things better. It is the happy heart that has the most courage; it is the joyous soul that has the greatest power; and it is the presence of sunshine that keeps darkness and gloom away.

When things go wrong, do not become disheartened; it is much easier to set them right when your soul is full of sunshine; so just be glad. It is the best way out.

When all seems lost, remember that it requires strength to regain everything; and it is the glad heart that remains strong. When the heart saddens, weakness will overtake you, and it will not be possible to regain your position. So therefore be glad regardless of what may transpire. It is one of the royal paths to everything that life holds dear.

But sadness does not merely bring weakness, it also brings illness, and age, and it shortens the length of our days. In gladness, however, there is

health and youth, strength and lon-
gevity. The glad heart will not grow
old, nor can illness ever enter where
the spirit of joy is supreme.

When in pain, be glad; and you can.
Be glad that you are greater than pain.
Be glad that pain has come to prevent
you from going wrong. Be glad that
you can prevent all pain in the future.
And be glad that it is wholly impossi-
ble for pain to come any more after
gladness has become the rule of your
life.

For your own advancement, be glad.
The spirit of joy is the spirit that
makes the heart kind, the soul strong
and the mind brilliant. It is this spirit
that makes for greatness, for noble-
ness, for excellence, for worth. We
repeat it, therefore, just be glad.

Would you be a pleasure and a delight to others, then be glad always.

And would you add to the measure of
your own joy, then give all the joy
you can to the largest possible number. This you can do by living more
and more in the spirit of that joy that
is in itself the essence of real joy. And
it is better to become the living in-
carnation of this spirit than to possess
all the wealth in the world. It is better to have attained to perpetual gladness than to have become the crowned
monarch of an entire solar system.
The reason is simple. The glad heart
is the sunshine of all life, a benedic-
tion to every man, a perpetual blessing to everything in creation.

Inspire every atom in your own
being to thrill with the spirit of joy;
not the joy of sentiment, but the joy
of strength, of triumph, of victory—
the joy that inwardly feels its power
sublime as the soul ascends in mas-
terful mien to the splendor of empy-

rean heights. It is such a joy that makes life a power, a blessing, an inspiration. And it is such a joy that comes perpetually to him who causes his soul to repeat again and again, that sweet reassuring refrain—just be glad.

Sing ever the song of triumph, of victory, of freedom—the song that declares the supremacy of the spirit over all that may be temporal or wrong. Sing the song of the soul rising above adversity or loss, proclaiming its freedom over all that is or is to be. When the soul continues to sing in this triumphant manner, all the elements of life follow the music of that which is always well; and in such a spirit everything must be always well.

Be glad, and smile with the smile that is sincere, the smile that shines just as sweetly and as naturally as the sunbeam. It is such a smile that

27

is a smile indeed; it is such a smile that comes from the soul—from the soul that is ever singing—just be glad. And how soon such a smile can change the world.

Meet adversity with such a smile; charm away tribulation with such a smile bursting forth into song; and let the music of the soul restore peace, love and harmony where these might have been absent. Then be stronger than adversity; rise superior to tribulation, and know that you are infinitely greater than all that is unfortunate or wrong.

In the midst of adversity combine strength with rejoicing, and fate must change. Before that music of the soul that is so high and so strong that it stirs the depth of every soul, all the world pays homage on a bended knee. And wisely, because such a power can change anything, transform anything, elevate anything, emancipate anything.

Go forth therefore into life with strength in your soul and music in your soul, and the future shall steadily and surely shape itself to comply with your dearest wishes and your highest aspirations.   Array yourself in the strength of truth, conviction, courage, faith, resolution, victory and triumph; and add to these another raiment—the music of gladness—and yours will be a life filled with glory, power and light.

The spirit of gladness when combined with the spirit of strength, will enlarge the mind, expand the soul, and enrich all thought and life; it is the moving mystery from within that makes everything good in human nature grow; that makes man noble and great; that makes human existence a world of immeasurable richness and sublime worth.   It is the same spirit that makes life "a thing of beauty and a joy forever;" that makes the lovely and the true become the tangible and the real; that causes all things we have loved so much come forth into our world in abundance. Therefore be glad when you feel strong, and be strong when you feel glad; and always know that you can.

Whatever your present position may be, there is a way from where you now stand that leads to better things and greater things for you than you ever knew. So whatever happens, just be glad. Live in the spirit of gladness; think in the spirit of joy; thus you will be able to see the royal path, for the mind that is illumined with gladness is never in the dark, never under the clouds of doubt or dismay.

When overtaken with calamity or tribulation, come forth undaunted and undismayed. Inspire the soul to reach

for the high realms of victory and joy;
and hold fast to that lofty position even
though the whole world seem to disappear beneath your feet. With such
a victory for your strong inspiration,
your own soul will prove more than
sufficient for all that life may demand
of you.

Then remember that mankind stands
ready to welcome and exalt every soul
whose strength is greater than any circumstance, whose joy is greater than
any tribulation, and whose faith is
greater than all doubts and failures in
the world.

When your plans cannot be carried
through at present, do not feel downcast or discouraged. Just be glad.
Give gladness to your mind and you
give clearness to your mind; and a
clear mind can see how to evolve better plans.

31

When your dreams do not come true
and your ideals do not become real,
refuse to be sad or disconsolate. Instead, rejoice with great joy to know
that you are greater than your dreams,
and wholly sufficient unto yourself regardless of what may transpire in the
real or the ideal. Thus you will give
expression to that greater power within you which surely can make your
ideals real and make all your dreams
come true.

Prove that your cherished dreams
are not necessary to your happiness,
and all of those dreams will come true.
Prove that you do not need the things
you want, and you will get them, pro-
vided of course that you give all that
is in you to the life you live. Prove
that you already are sufficient in yourself, and have sufficient in the richness
of your own world, and more and more
will gather for you, both in the within

and in the without. It is much gathering more; much in the within gathering more everywhere; it is your own strength inspiring all things to come with strength; it is the spirit of the great life aroused in yourself causing all things of greatness and worth to come and gather in the entire world of your own life. And it is in this spirit that we live and move and have our being, when the soul continues to sing that sweet reassuring refrain—just be glad.

Whatever may be, therefore, or come to pass, continue in the spirit of this refrain. For to live in the music of such a refrain is to enjoy life infinitely more than it was ever enjoyed before. And that in itself is much indeed. Besides, be glad whatever happens, and something better will happen. When the good happens, let the soul sing with rejoicing; then greater good will happen, and there will be cause for greater rejoicing. When that which is not good happens, let the soul sing in the same triumphant spirit, and the power of that spirit will cause all ills to vanish as darkness before the glory of the morn.

Remove the cause of sadness by giving all the elements of life to the spirit of joy. Smile away the darkness and the gloom; sing away the discord and the pain; banish tribulation with rejoicing; then you may in truth be joyous and be glad; and every hour of your long and triumphant life will add new evidence to that great inspiring statement—**all things respond to the call of rejoicing; all things gather where life is a song.**

HETHER we believe that life was made for happiness or that happiness was made for life, matters not. The fact remains that he alone can live the most and enjoy the best who takes for his motto—just be glad. Whatever comes, or whatever may fail to come, this one thing he will always remember— just be glad. Though every mind in the world may give darkness, his will continue to give light; and though all may be lost, so there seems nothing more to give, he will not forget to give happiness.

The one great thing to do under every circumstance and in the midst of every event is this—just be glad. Wherever you may be, add sunshine. Whatever your position may be, be also a human sunbeam. What a difference when the sunbeam comes in;

then why should the sunbeam remain
without?

There is a sunbeam in every heart.
Why hide it at any time? Does not the
world need your smiles? Is not everybody made happier and better when in
the presence of a radiant countenance?
Do we ever forget the face that shines
as the sun? And does not such a mem-
ory continue to give us strength and
inspiration all through the turnings
and complexities of life? We are not
here to give sadness, but joy. We were
not made to hide our souls in a dark
thunder cloud, but to let the spirit
shine in all its splendor and beauty.
We are made to make life an endless
song, and the sweet refrain of that
beautiful song is—just be glad.

When things go wrong, just be glad.
It is sunshine that brings forth the
flowers from the cold and soggy earth.
It is light-heartedness that puts to

flight the burdens of life. It is the
smile of human sweetness that dispels the chilly night of isolation and
brings friendship and love to the
bosom of the yearning soul. Then
why be sad when gladness can do so
much? Why be sad for a single mo-
ment when the smile of a single mo-
ment has the power even to change
the course of human destiny. We all
remember how soon a smile of God
can change the world. Why not always live in that magical smile and
just be glad? **Then we should remember that all things respond to the song
of rejoicing; all things gather where
life is a song.**

Do you think that life is too difficult
for smiles, and that you have too much
to pass through to ever have happiness? Then remember that the glad
heart knows no difficulty. The sunbeam even smiles at darkness, and

converts the blackness of the storm into a brilliant rainbow. Just be glad, and your tears shall also become a bow of promise; yes, and more, for in that promise you shall discern the unmistakable signs of a brighter day upon the coming morn.

Do not think that happiness must keep its distance so long as you have so much to pass through. The more you have to pass through, the more you need happiness. It is the shining countenance that never turns back; it is the glad heart that finds strength to go on; it is the mind with the most sunshine that can see the most clearly where to go and how to act that the goal in view may be gained.

Just be glad, and half the burden is gone. Just be glad, and your work becomes mostly pleasure. Just be glad, and you take the keenest delight in

meeting even the greatest of obstacles
and the most difficult of problems.

When you meet reverses, just be
glad; for do we not again remember
how soon a smile of God can change
the world? It is not gloom that dispels darkness; it is not disconsolance
that makes the mind brilliant and the
soul strong. But if we would turn the
tide of ill fortune we need all our bril-
liancy and all our strength. To master
fate, to conquer destiny, to make life
our own, we must be all there is in us
to be. Then we must remember that
it is sunshine that makes the flowers
grow, and that transforms the acorn
into a great and massive oak. Everything in nature, and in man, the crown-
ing glory of nature, responds with
pleasure to the magic touch of the
smiling sunbeam. For again we must
remember that all things respond to

the call of rejoicing; all things gather where life is a song.

Promise yourself that whatever may come you will always remember—just be glad. When good things come into life, gladness will make them better. When things come that should not have come, gladness will so brighten your mind that you can see clearly how to turn everything to good account. Whatever happens or not, just be glad, and it will be much better than it possibly could have been otherwise. Therefore, gladness is not a mere sentiment. It pays. It is not a luxury for the favored few alone. It is a necessity that all should secure in abundance.

If it is your belief that there is nothing in your life for which you can justly be glad, stop and count your blessings. You will surprise yourself; and you will then and there resolve never to depreciate yourself again. Henceforth, you will find it easier to be glad; and you will also find that the more things you are glad for, the more things you will have to be glad for. Gladness is a magnet and it draws more and more of everything that can increase gladness. Just be glad—always and under every circumstance, and nothing shall be withheld from you that can add to your welfare and happiness.

Should you find it easy to be glad when things go right, and difficult to be glad when things go wrong, you are not creating your own sunshine; and it is only the sunshine that we create ourselves, in our own world, that makes things grow in our own world. Be glad because you want to be glad, regardless of events, and you will have found that fountain of joy within that is ever ready to overflow. Be glad at all times because it is best to be glad at all times; and be glad in the presence of everything because gladness makes it better for everything.

Just be glad, and the world will be kind to you. The sunbeam has no occasion for regrets. It is always welcome; it is always loved. Just be glad, and you will have friends without number; and it is he who has many friends—friends that are good and true, who finds everything that is rich and beautiful in human existence. Just be glad, and you will be sought for, far and wide. The world is not looking for gloom and depression; it is looking for sunshine and joy.

Just be glad, even though the whole world be against you, and all the elements of nature be in a conspiracy to place you in the hands of destruction. Even at such a time, just be glad. Thus you prove your strength. And he who can prove that he is stronger than any adversary, will win the respect—yes, and the friendship, of every adversary. What was against you will be for you. And this was your secret—you refused to be downcast, you refused to weaken, you refused to be less than your greatest self—even when everything seemed lost, you were strong enough to be true to all that you knew to be true, and you tuned your life to the music of that sweetest of all refrains—just be glad. Because you were glad, even when there was nothing to make you glad, you proved that you deserved everything that has the power to make you glad. And that which we truly deserve must come to remain as our own.

Just be glad. Whether there is anything to be glad for or not, just be glad. It is the royal path to happiness.

JUST BE GLAD

It is the royal path to all that is worthy and beautiful in life. Above all things, possess gladness, and you will soon possess those things that produce gladness. Be your own sunbeam, and you will attract a million sunbeams. Be your own source of your own joy, and you will attract everything and everybody that can add to your joy. To him that hath shall be given. And he already hath who has found the riches of his own nature. To find those riches is the first step. All else must follow. All other things will be added. And to find those riches, use well every talent you possess. Then whatever comes, just be glad. **For all things respond to the call of rejoicing; all things gather where life is a song.**